FUSION READING

THE SUMMARIZATION STRATEGY

McGraw Hill Education

Bothell, WA • Chicago, IL • Columbus, OH • New York, NY

www.mheonline.com

The *McGraw-Hill* Companies

Education

Send all inquiries to:
McGraw-Hill Education
130 E. Randolph, Suite 400
Chicago, IL 60601

ISBN: 978-0-07-662711-0
MHID: 0-07-662711-X
Printed in the United States of America.

3 4 5 6 7 8 9 QDB 16 15 14 13 12

The Summarization Strategy

Table of Contents

Summarization Passages continued

Summarization Comprehension Tests cont.

TSS Practice Record Form

"Preview the Selection" Step

Partner							
	Passage #						
	Score						
	Attempt	1	2	3	4	5	6
Individual	Passage #						
	Score						
	Attempt	1	2	3	4	5	6

"Paraphrase Each Paragraph" Step

Partner							
	Passage #						
	Score						
	Attempt	1	2	3	4	5	6
Individual	Passage #						
	Score						
	Attempt	1	2	3	4	5	6

"Summarize the Selection" Step

Partner							
	Passage #						
	Score						
	Attempt	1	2	3	4	5	6
Individual	Passage #						
	Score						
	Attempt	1	2	3	4	5	6

The Summarization Strategy Progress Chart

Name: _____

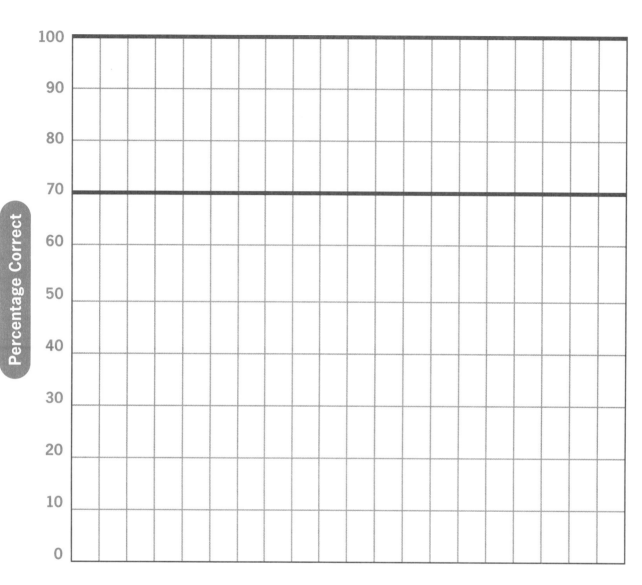

(Write the passage number on the blank line.)

Progress Chart Key

✱ = Strategy Use Score (Mastery = 100%)

● = Comprehension Score (Mastery = 70%)

Circle the number of all passages practiced with your teacher.

Leaving a Fire

by Marna Lee

The time to **plan** for a fire emergency is before it happens. This is when everyone is calm and thinking clearly. This is when decisions about safe escape routes can be discussed and made. Have a family meeting. Don't delay. It's too late to plan after a fire starts.

Knowing ahead of time how to get out during a fire can save lives. The best way out in a fire is the route you use to go in and out every day. Yet, in a fire this route may be blocked. Be sure to plan other escape routes.

Take each person to his or her room and describe what to do in case of fire. Give everyone a job. Older children should take care of younger ones. Plans may have to be made for anyone who cannot escape without help. Adults who can't walk should sleep on the first floor. Small children should sleep near older persons who can help them. Only healthy, able persons should sleep in hard-to-reach attics or basements.

Practice your escape plan at night when it is dark. This will help you decide whether your plan will work well. If it does not, then revise your plan. For instance, make sure that a child can actually open the window he or she is supposed to use for escape. Teach children to close their bedroom doors. Tell them to wait by an open window until someone can reach them from outside. Children should be taught that if an adult cannot be awakened, the children must leave by themselves. Choose a meeting place outside. This way you can tell whether everyone is safely out of the building. Know where nearby telephones or fire alarm boxes are found.

If you live in an apartment, learn where the **fire alarm** is in the building. Your family should know what the fire alarm bell sounds like. They should know what to do when they hear it. Try to get the other families together to have fire drills. Write down the telephone number of the fire department. Tape the number to each phone. Don't forget to let the babysitter in on your plans. Tell your babysitter what to do in case of fire.

Early warning is the key to a safe escape from a fire. It has been shown time and time again that a family can escape when warned early enough.

Backpacking

by Marna Lee

Countless people today enjoy the pleasures and benefits of mountain hiking. Backpacking offers freedom found in no other type of wilderness travel. However, you must know what to expect when you hike off into the wilderness. There will be no running water or shelters to use. There will be no tables to eat from and no grills to hold your pots and pans. There will be few trail signs to guide you. You must know how to follow a map. You will be on your own.

Still, there are countless **places** you can go. Try an overnight trip to a mountain or stream. Follow a marked trail that seems inviting. A trial run will help tone up muscles and show mistakes in plans. During a short trip, you will not suffer too badly if something has been left at home.

Experienced backpackers pride themselves on being able to **travel light.** With many, weight saving is a game. Some cut towels in half and saw the handles off toothbrushes to save ounces. They measure out just the right amount of food needed and put it in plastic bags. Plastic bags are lighter than cardboard. There are dozens of tricks to save ounces that add up to pounds.

Footwear is an important thing to keep in mind. Sneakers are cool and cheap. For youngsters who are growing, the heavy-soled, ankle-high sneaker is best. Rubber is good where the going is wet. Hikers in swamps and bogs prefer the shoepac above anything else. However, **leather** is the most popular shoe material for all-around hiking. It wears well and is soft. It can be waterproofed to shed snow and rain.

Leather soles on boots are slippery. Most hikers use rubber or cord soles. When the soles wear out, thick rubber lug soles can be put on. These grip the rocks well.

Hiking boots should fit comfortably over two pairs of socks, one thin and one thick. They should protect the ankles and support the foot. They have to withstand long distances, sometimes on rocks and roots. Be sure that boots are well broken in before the trip. A mountain trail is no place to break in a new pair of boots. Only boots made for hiking should be used; ski boots are for skiing and cowboy boots are for horseback riding. Footwear with eyelets and lacing has proved best for hiking. A wise hiker always brings an extra pair of laces.

A Family of PLANETS

by Marna Lee

There are seven planets besides Earth in the sun's family. The word *planet* means "wanderer." When the people of ancient times studied the sky, they gave names to the groups of stars they saw. They learned to know the stars that made up each group. They saw some "stars," however, that did not stay in any one group. These "stars" came to be called wanderers, or planets. Finally, people realized that these stars were not stars at all, but bodies, like Earth, that keep traveling around the sun. They seem to wander from star group to star group because of their journeys around the sun.

Planets look to people like stars, but they are really very different. Stars are very, very hot. They shine with their own light. Planets do not shine with their own light. They shine only because the sun is shining on them. Moonlight, as most people know, is secondhand sunlight. The moon merely reflects the light that shines on it from the sun. The light from planets is secondhand sunlight, too.

Of the seven other planets, only five can be seen with the naked eye. People of ancient times knew of only five "wandering stars." The other planets were not discovered until after telescopes were invented. The planets that are visible without a telescope are Mercury, Venus, Mars, Jupiter, and Saturn. The others are Uranus and Neptune.

The path of a planet is called its **orbit.** The planets keep traveling in their same orbits around the sun century after century. They do not stray from their path because the sun is pulling them with so much force that they cannot escape. Scientists call the power with which the sun is pulling the planets the **force of gravitation.** Often this force is called gravity for short.

It would seem that if the sun is pulling the planets with so much force, the planets would fall into the sun. They do not because they are moving too fast. Each planet moves with a speed that just balances the pull of the sun. The outer planets move more slowly than those closer to the sun.

Many of the planets have moons that travel around them as they travel around the sun. Earth has one moon. Mercury and Venus have none. Jupiter, in contrast, has twelve moons. Mars and Neptune have two. Uranus has five and Saturn has nine.

Alfred the Great

by Marna Lee

The course of **English history** would have been very different had it not been for King Alfred. He won renown as both a political leader and a warrior. He is justly called "the Great." The England of Alfred's time was made up of four small Saxon kingdoms. The strongest was Wessex, in the south. Alfred was born in about 848, the youngest son of the king of Wessex. Each of Alfred's three older brothers, in turn, ruled the kingdom. Alfred was by temperament a scholar. His health was never robust.

Nevertheless, in his early youth Alfred fought with his brother Ethelred against **Danish invaders.** Alfred was 23 when Ethelred died, but he had already won the confidence of the army. He was at once proclaimed king. By this time, the Danes had penetrated to all parts of the island. One after the other, three of the Saxon kingdoms had fallen to the Danish invaders. Under Alfred's leadership, the Saxons again found courage. The worst crisis came in the winter of 877, when the Danish king invaded Wessex with his army. In 878, Alfred was defeated at Chippenham. He was forced to go into hiding.

A few months later, Alfred forced a Danish surrender at Chippenham. The Danes agreed to a boundary between Alfred's kingdom and the Danish lands to the north. The treaty, however, did not ensure permanent peace. The Danes attacked London and the coastal towns repeatedly. In about 896, the Danes finally admitted defeat. They stopped trying to gain a foothold in southern England.

Alfred was much more than the defender of his country. He took a keen interest in law and order. He was concerned with improving the cultural standards of his people. He encouraged industries of all kinds. He rebuilt London, which had been partly destroyed by the Danes. He collected and revised the old laws of the kingdom. He invited learned men from other countries to instruct the people. The "books most necessary for all men to know" were translated from Latin into English so that the people might read them. Alfred himself took a part in preparing the translations.

Alfred died at the age of about 51 in 899. He was not a true king of England, for he ruled less than half of the island. After his death, however, his capable son, Edward the Elder, and his grandsons extended their rule over all of England.

Tracking the Emperor Goose

by Marna Lee

Why are people tracking the wild goose? Why would anyone want to? One kind of wild goose is called the **Emperor Goose.** It is spied upon, followed, and watched. Every move that it makes is noticed and carefully written down. But don't feel sorry for the Emperor Goose. It's all for the goose's own good.

Little is know about this goose. It is a lovely and rare North American waterfowl. Because this goose is so rare, researchers want to be sure that it will survive. To do this, they have to know and understand its habits.

The known nesting place of the Emperor Goose is small. It is found in a semiwild part of the state of Alaska. The land around **Kokechik Bay** seems to attract the bird. The streams of the Yukon Delta empty into the bay. These same streams carry pollution to the nesting sites, especially after a storm. The researchers want to learn how human behavior affect the birds. First, however, people must know something about the goose itself.

To find answers to questions, researchers have set up camps near the breeding grounds. After locating and studying the nests, scientists have learned many things. For example, they now know how the female guards her nest. She presses close to the ground. She stretches her neck out and remains quite still. In this way, she looks like a piece of driftwood. And who would bother with a piece of driftwood?

Scientists have also learned that after the Emperor Geese mate, they stay together. While the female sits on the eggs, the male stands or feeds nearby. At times, the male may wander off a little way. He is sure to come back quickly if the female is disturbed.

When the eggs hatch, the young geese are a dark gray color. After two weeks, the dark gray turns to a light gray. When the goslings reach the fledgling stage, they take on a blue tone. The adult goose can be recognized by the whiteness of its head and the back of its neck. This white contrasts with the black of its throat. Its silver-gray feathers and its bright yellow-orange feet make this bird one of the most colorful geese.

Scientists need to know a lot more about the Emperor Goose. The researchers in Alaska hope to add to their knowledge in order to protect this amazing bird.

Building the Pyramids

by Marna Lee

The pyramids and other tombs were built on the west bank of the Nile River. The Egyptians chose the west bank as the "land of the dead" because that was where the dying sun disappeared each evening.

The building of the pyramids was generally started during the dry season of May and June. That was when the Nile River was at its lowest level. The crops of the year before had been harvested. The ground was dry and cracked under a baking sun. The farmers had no work to do in the fields.

The **farmers** became pyramid builders. They were paid for their labor in food and clothing. The workers were provided with tools. There were no coins or other types of money used in Egypt at that time. Many of the farmers probably worked on the pyramids of their own free will rather than as forced labor. The work was a means of adding to their livelihood.

Once the Nile flood began, barges were able to bring stones down the river from the distant quarries. The stones could be unloaded close to the building sites at the desert's edge. However, most of the stone used in the pyramids came from the surrounding desert itself. On land, the stones were transported on sleds with wide wooden runners. Wheels probably would have been useless. They would have sunk at once into the sand.

Every step of the work was accomplished with *human labor.* The huge blocks of stone were cut and shaped by hand. Tools of flint or copper were used. The Egyptians had no iron. The stones were lifted and hauled onto the sleds with the help of wooden wedges. Stout wooden bars were used as levers. The sleds themselves were not pulled by animals but by teams of men. The oxen and donkeys that the Egyptians used for fieldwork could not have been fed and watered in the harsh desert.

As the pyramid grew taller, the blocks of stone were pulled uphill on ramps made of rocks, sand, and mud. Logs, laid crosswise on the ramps, were embedded in the mud every few feet. They acted as stoppers to keep the heavy loads from slipping backward. Any interior rooms or passages had to be finished before the upper part of the pyramid was completed.

Altogether about 80 pyramids were built as burying places for the kings of Egypt.

COLORS

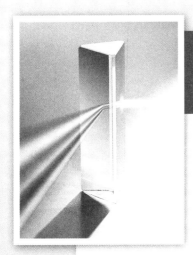

by Marna Lee

One of the most striking features of the visible world is the abundance of color. The sky can be blue or black or gray or even reddish or purplish. Soils can be black or brown or gray or even red. Bodies of water look blue or green.

One of the important ways people obtain information about the world is by looking at the colors of things. When the green leaves of a plant turn brown, it may be a sign that the plant is sick. It can also signal the season of the year. In the autumn, the leaves of many trees turn brown.

The color of a fruit can reveal whether it is ripe. A green banana is unripe; a yellow one is ripe. A yellow banana with brown and black spots is overripe. A green tomato is unripe, but a red one is ripe. Color can also indicate the flavor of foods. Brown rice has a different flavor from that of white rice.

What does it mean to say that a tomato is red? Is color part of the tomato in the same way that shape is? A tomato examined in the dark is still perceived as round but not as being red. It has no color at all. Moreover, if a bright blue light is shone only on the tomato, it does not look red but black. So color, unlike shape, **depends on light.** In fact, it cannot exist apart from light.

Light from the noontime sun looks white. But if a ray of white light is aimed at a prism, a broad band of different colors looking like a rainbow emerges. This color array is called the visible spectrum.

In the seventeenth century, *Isaac Newton* discovered that a second prism could not add more color to light that had already passed through a prism. Red stayed red, green stayed green, and so on. But he observed that the second prism could spread the colors of the spectrum farther apart. A narrow red beam entering the second prism would emerge as a wider band of red. Newton also found that if he turned the second prism upside down, white light would emerge. From these experiments he concluded that white light is a mixture of many different colors. A **prism** is somehow able to bend it in such a way that the individual colors separate.

Machines for TRANSPORTATION

by Marna Lee

Transportation is something that touches everyone's life. Machines play an ever-increasing role in it. Trucks carry goods along the highways. Jets streak across the United States in about four hours. Great liners plow the seas at impressive speeds. Diesel trains roar over the rails from the Atlantic to the Pacific.

Today most people take transportation machines for granted. It was not so long ago, however, that people didn't have these machines. At first, everyone walked and carried loads on his or her back. Then people began to train animals. Soon travelers could ride horses, camels, or donkeys. Pack animals carried their baggage.

After the invention of the **wheel,** people built carts and wagons. With these wheeled vehicles, much larger loads could be carried. Still, for hundreds of years, land transportation was limited by the speed and strength of some draft animal.

Meanwhile, seafarers had known for centuries how to harness the **wind.** As time passed, shipwrights learned how to build bigger and faster sailing ships. Even so, when there was no wind, the nineteenth-century clipper ship captain was no better off than the ancient Egyptian on a Nile barge.

Then, in 1829, George Stephenson from England thought of mounting one of the new steam engines on a set of wheels. His little locomotive was able to pull a train of small cars along a track at about 20 miles (32 kilometers) an hour. This was faster than anyone had ever traveled over land before. The **railroad age** had dawned.

At about the same time, American inventor Robert Fulton mounted a steam engine in a boat. The engine turned a pair of paddle wheels. Steamboats were soon puffing up and down all of the great rivers. They carried passengers and freight from town to town.

Steamboats were used on the seas, too. Paddle-wheel ocean steamers always carried masts and sails in case they ran out of wood. Later, screw-propeller vessels, which burned coal, were used.

The steam engine became so improved that it seemed it would forever remain the chief means of powering transportation machines. But then the gasoline engine was invented. Instead of getting power from expanding steam, this engine worked by explosions of gasoline vapor. The gas engine opened the door for the modern automobile, truck, and airplane. Yet, the gas engine would soon meet stiff competition from the diesel engine. Together they would power most means of modern transportation.

A Pet Parakeet

by Marna Lee

Few pets are as popular as parakeets, also called **budgies.** These are small parrots native to tropical regions. The beautifully colored little bird is a fine pet for shut-ins and people who live in apartments. Its friendliness and playfulness make it a lively companion.

With patience, you can teach almost any parakeet to talk. Usually a young parakeet is easier to train than a mature bird. When you bring your budgie home, let it stay in its cage from one to two weeks until you see that it is used to its new surroundings and to you.

At first, your pet may not be able to find the food cup. Spread seed liberally among the gravel on the floor of the cage. Feed your budgie once a day. When it learns to eat from the cup, empty the waste hulls daily. Be sure it has grit. It also likes little extras in its treat cup, such as millet seed, a bit of greens, a piece of apple, and finely chopped egg.

When a budgie becomes tame in its cage, you can finger-train it. You may start by talking quietly to it as you slowly and repeatedly put your hand in its cage, near the bottom. It will come to sit on your finger. Then you can train it to stay on a playpen, a wood tray with sides raised to keep gravel from spilling. You can fit it with a variety of toys, such as bells, ladders, a seesaw, and a trapeze.

To teach your bird to talk, begin training it as soon as it is **cage-tame.** A budgie learns faster when it is the only bird. Some people cover the cage while they speak to the bird so that it will concentrate on the voice. A budgie seems to find **words starting with *p* and *b*** the easiest to learn. Stand at the cage and, in your normal tone, clearly say a simple phrase such as "pretty bird." Repeat several times a day, if possible, or at least five minutes each morning and night. Only when your pet has learned that one phrase should you teach it another.

Some budgies talk after two months of training. Others may take six months. Many people use parakeet recordings for teaching. Others prefer to train by their own voices, for the bird imitates the tone of its trainer. Some parakeets learn hundreds of words.

PHOTO: Juniors Bildarchiv/Alamy

Copyright © University of Kansas

People's BEST Friend

by Marna Lee

The dog is one of the most popular pets in the world. It ordinarily remains loyal to a considerate master, and because of this trait, the dog has been called a **person's best friend.** Class distinctions between people have no part in a dog's life. It can be a faithful companion to either rich or poor. Dogs have been domesticated for most of human history and have thus endeared themselves to many over the years. Stories have been told about brave dogs that served admirably in war or that risked their lives to save people in danger.

A dog fits easily into family life. It thrives on praise and affection. When a master tells a dog that it is good, the animal happily wags its tail. But when a master scolds a dog, it skulks away with a sheepish look and with its tail tucked between its legs. People in cities as well as those in other areas can enjoy a dog. Medium-size or small dogs are best suited for confined city living. Large dogs need considerable exercise over a large area and thrive best in the country.

When a person decides to own a dog, he or she should be prepared to **care** for it properly. For a dog to stay healthy, it must be correctly fed and adequately groomed. Also, its medical needs must be met. For a dog to be well-mannered, it must be properly trained. It should never be ill-treated or mishandled. Otherwise, it will bite in its own defense.

The **wild ancestors** of all dogs were hunters. Wolves and other wild relatives of the dog still hunt in packs for their food. Dogs have retained the urge to be with the pack. This is why they do not like to be left alone for long. Some breeds of dogs still retain the hunting instinct.

Dogs exist in a wide range of sizes, colors, and temperaments. Some, such as the Doberman pinscher and the German shepherd, serve as alert and aggressive watchdogs. Others, such as the beagle and the cocker spaniel, are playful family pets, even though they were bred for hunting. Still others, such as the collie and the Welsh corgi, can herd farm or range animals. Each of the dogs mentioned is a purebred. However, a mongrel dog, one with many breeds in its background, can just as easily fit into family life.

A Desert Fox

by Marna Lee

When you think of the desert, you may think of thirst. But thirst is not the only problem facing those who live in deserts. Water alone will not sustain life. For animals in the desert, hunger and the search for food consume a major part of their daily lives. Because the desert can be a hostile place, animals living there have adapted in special ways that help them find food. One such animal is the little **kit fox.**

The kit fox is about the size and weight of a large house cat. It resembles its distant cousin, the gray fox. Both have thick coats and bushy tails. But the fur of the kit fox is buff yellow or gray, with black-tipped hairs. It becomes a perfect disguise for slipping around in the desert moonlight. The kit fox ranges over nearly the whole western desert in the United States. But it is rarely seen, and never in daylight. Anyone who spends time in the desert may, from time to time, catch a glimpse of the kit fox and find its tracks in the sand.

Kit foxes are unafraid and rather curious about people, yet they remain shy. They live underground in burrows that may extend up to 8 feet (2.4 meters). There the kit fox spends the hot part of each day. Once a year the young, called kittens, are born in the burrows. Usually kit foxes have four or five kittens in a litter.

The kit fox feeds on any small animals it can find, but its favorite is the kangaroo rat. The **kangaroo rat** has been called the "staff of life" for the kit fox. Rat burrows that have been dug open by foxes can be found in sandy areas. The kit foxes eat wood rats, pocket mice, small birds, lizards, and insects, too.

Smells vanish quickly in dry desert winds. Instead of a keen sense of smell, the successful hunter needs **acute hearing.** The kit fox's ears are much larger in proportion to its size than the ears of other foxes. They are broad and pointed. Its ears can be moved independently, allowing the kit fox to listen in two directions at once. At the slightest sound, its ears twitch, listening for the direction of prey. Then the animal turns toward the sound, moving swiftly on its short, sturdy legs. The kit fox's ears are a helpful adaptation to desert life.

BUILDING A 10-SPEED

by Marna Lee

United States manufacturers produce more kinds of 10-speed bicycles than any other type of bike. The price of a 10-speed ranges from about $100 to $3,000. Price varies with the quality of the parts and the material used for the frame. The amount of handwork needed to construct the bike is another factor.

A cyclist may have a 10-speed bike **custom built.** The frame builder designs the bike to fit the person's height, arm length, and inside leg measurement. The designer also chooses the parts that make up the bike. The type of cycling for which it will be used must also be considered. A custom-built bike can be constructed to provide the maximum speed for every ounce of energy used by the rider. Most bikes, however, are made to conventional standards in sizes indicated by the wheel diameter.

A quality 10-speed bike is often constructed of **lightweight high-carbon steel;** however, some frames produced in the 1980s were made of plastic. The steel frame provides strength, rigidity, lightness, and responsiveness. The best frames are butted; that is, they are thick at the ends to give the bike stiffness and strength, and thinner in the middle for lightness.

The first step in frame construction for a 10-speed bike is to polish and connect the metal tubes of the frame. The builder cuts an exact curve into the ends of the tubes so that they fit together precisely.

PHOTO: Andersen Ross/Digital Vision/Getty Images

The tubes are joined by a device called a lug. Then they are fitted and held together by means of brazing. This operation requires extremely high temperatures. If not done expertly, brazing can weaken the metal.

The new frame is cleaned with blasts of compressed air. Excess joining material around the lugs is filed away by hand and the corners are smoothed. Next, each joint is inspected. Finally, the frame is examined for proper alignment.

A quality bicycle frame often receives five coats of paint: undercoat, primer, base coat, top coat, and, finally, lacquer. Then the front and rear forks are painted and fitted to the frame. Finally, the frame is clamped upside down and fitted with brakes, gears, handlebars, chainset, seat, pedals, and, lastly, wheels. The new bike is now ready for riding.

The Florida Keys

by Marna Lee

The small islands off the coast of Florida are called keys. From Spanish, the word *key* means "rock" or "islet." The name *Florida Keys* refers to the chain of about 60 keys that extends from Miami Beach to Key West.

The eastern end of the chain is a remnant of an old coral reef. Living corals are still building reefs in the area. The western keys are made of limestone. Mangrove thickets line the shores and cover some of the low islands. The growth that rises on the higher ground is composed of tropical hardwoods and palms. Some small keys are submerged at high tide.

The largest of the keys is **Key Largo.** John Pennekamp Coral Reef State Park is located in the Atlantic waters off this key. Its chief attractions are underwater scenery and living coral formations. Settlements have sprung up on some of the larger keys. There is little agriculture because of the thin soil. Fishing resorts entertain people who come for deep-sea fishing.

The southernmost city in the United States, outside of Hawaii, is Key West. It spreads over a small island. It lies some 100 miles (160 kilometers) southwest of the mainland. The island is the westernmost in the Florida Keys. Its location provides sunny year-round warmth. Its shores are bathed by warm Gulf Stream water, and the southeast trade winds bring mild breezes.

Key West's history has been colorful. Spanish adventurers of the sixteenth century were early settlers. Pirate ships hid in the passes and waterways between the keys. The offshore reefs still hold the sunken wrecks of ships lost in sea battles long ago.

The settlement on Key West became a city in 1828. Cuban cigar makers arrived and became successful. Sponge fishing was good. During the 1890s, Key West was Florida's largest city.

Since 1938, the *Overseas Highway* has linked Key West to Miami, 155 miles (249 kilometers) away. Many tourists use the highway to come to the island city. Hotels, motels, and other tourist facilities have been built. Today the tourist trade, the naval air station, and fishing provide the greatest employment. Shrimp are caught in the Gulf of Mexico. Giant sea crayfish are sold as lobsters. A cannery turns sea turtles into green turtle soup.

An aqueduct (pipeline for water) has been built by the federal government to supply badly needed fresh water to Key West and the other islands.

THE AMOEBA

by Marna Lee

The smallest unit of living matter that can exist by itself is the *cell*. All cells consist of protoplasm, the "living jelly." The protoplasm of a typical cell forms three parts—the cell membrane, the cytoplasm, and the nucleus. The membrane encloses the other cell structures. The bulk of the cell's chemical work takes place in the cytoplasm, which surrounds the nucleus—the control center of the cell.

The most primitive form of animal life is a microscopic creature composed of just one cell—the amoeba. The amoeba has two kinds of **cytoplasm:** at the surface, a stiff, gel-like cytoplasm forms a layer that acts like a membrane. It holds the inner, more watery cytoplasm and its contents together. The outer membrane is flexible, taking on the shape of the more watery cytoplasm inside, which is continually moving and changing the body shape of the amoeba. The name *amoeba* comes from a Greek word that means "change."

The amoeba travels by changing its body shape. It extends a portion of its body to form a temporary foot called a pseudopod, meaning "false foot." Then it slowly pulls the rest of its body into the pseudopod. The pseudopod enlarges to form the whole body. New pseudopods form as old ones disappear. The amoeba also uses its pseudopods to surround food, which it draws into its body. The food remains in a bubble-like chamber within the amoeba while it is digested. Water flows into and wastes flow out of the amoeba through the outer membrane. The amoeba also breathes through its membrane.

If an amoeba is cut apart, it instantly forms a new membrane over the cut surface. Only the part containing the nucleus has a chance of surviving. The nucleus is also necessary for reproduction. To reproduce, the nucleus pinches into two and the amoeba splits evenly in half. The process, called fission, takes less than one hour.

Although an amoeba has no nerves, it reacts to its surroundings. It retreats from strong light, or from water that is too hot or too cold. If touched or shaken, it rolls into a ball.

Amoebae dwell in fresh and salt waters, in moist soils, and in moist parts of other animals. Common species are found in ponds and puddles and even in the human intestine. Most amoebae that live in other animals are harmless, but some are responsible for serious diseases.

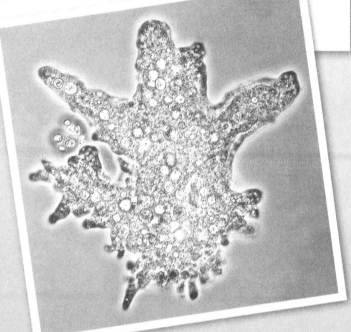

Take a **Deep** Breath

by Marna Lee

Food is vital to humans. They have to eat because food keeps them strong and active. Yet people have been known to live without food for several weeks. Water is even more important to humans. Without it, nobody can live for more than a few days. But even more important to human bodies than food and water is the air around them. They cannot live for more than a few minutes without breathing.

Humans usually breathe from **16 to 20 times each minute.** If you analyzed the air you breathe, you would find it is a mixture of different gases. Most of it—about four-fifths—is *nitrogen.* One-fifth is *oxygen.* There is also a tiny amount of *carbon dioxide,* a little water vapor (which gives air its humidity), and some traces of what are called rare gases.

If you were to put a bag over your nose and mouth to catch the air you breathe out, you would find some strange changes. There would still be the same amount of nitrogen. There would also be the same traces of rare gases. But there would be much less oxygen and a hundred times more carbon dioxide than in the air you breathed in. There would also be considerably more water vapor.

What happens is that each time you breathe, an exchange takes place. You keep some oxygen; you breathe out much more carbon dioxide and water vapor than you breathed in. The reason is that every moment of the day and night your body is using up energy. Your heart uses up energy as it beats. Your muscles use up energy. So does your brain, and so does every other part of you. All this energy is produced by the work of the millions and millions of cells that make up your body. Every one of these cells needs oxygen in order to do its work.

As the cells use up oxygen, they form **carbon dioxide.** This is a waste product, just as smoke and ashes are the waste products of a fire. The cells must get rid of this waste.

So your body carries out these two processes at the same time. You breathe in the oxygen that the cells need to produce energy. You breathe out the carbon dioxide that is harmful. It sounds so simple. Yet your life depends on these processes happening day and night without interruption.

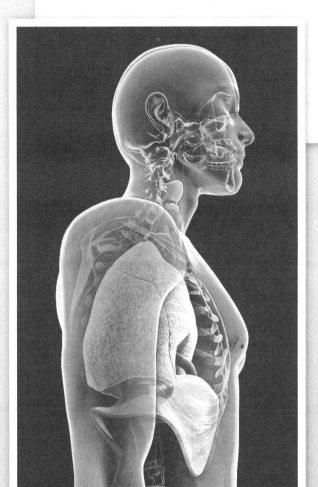

FLAX

by Marna Lee

Flax has been raised for thousands of years. Ancient Egyptian mummies were wrapped in linen, which is made from the fibers of the flax plant. Records show that humans have eaten flax products for centuries, often for medicinal purposes.

Cultivated flax is of *two types:* one is grown for *fiber production,* the other for *seed.* Fiber flax grows tall and has few branches. It needs a short, cool growing season with plenty of rainfall evenly distributed; otherwise, the plants become woody and the fiber is rough and dry. To harvest fiber flax, farmers pull the plants up by the roots because cutting injures the fibers. Flax-pulling machines are used in the United States. Elsewhere, low-cost hand labor is used, which makes the imported product cheaper. This is the chief reason for the limited production of fiber flax in the United States. After harvesting, the flax seed is separated from the straw in deseeding machines. Next, the flax is retted, or rotted, in a pool or tank of warm water. Retting takes from four to six days. The water helps bacteria on the plant penetrate the woody stems. The bacteria ferment and break down the pectins, which cement together the woody and fibrous portions of the plant. The retted flax is then dried in open fields.

Scutching is the next operation. This process extracts the fiber, loosened during retting, from the remainder of the plant. The flax fiber is then combed to grade it and prepare it for the spinner. This is usually done by hand, drawing the fibers over pins to straighten them and to remove short, tangled fibers.

The long-line fibers make the best linen cloth. Linen made from these kinds of fibers is strong, durable, and moisture absorbent. It has a high luster. It is also resistant to microorganisms and its smooth surface repels soil.

Seed flax is an important crop as well. Farmers harvest seed flax with a combination mower and thresher. They then ship the seed to a linseed market. It is used in paints and varnishes and in linoleum and oilcloth.

The straw from seed flax was once a waste material. Now it provides the paper for practically all the cigarettes that are made in the United States. Many other specialty papers also are produced from seed flax straw. It is also used in upholstery stuffing, insulating and packing material, and fiber rugs.

Everyday Life in
ANCIENT EGYPT

by Marna Lee

People today live in an age when every year brings forth new inventions and discoveries and new fads and fashions that affect everyday life. Through communications, migration, and travel, every culture can merge into new lifestyles.

The ancient Egyptians had their greatest creative period at the beginning of their long history. After that, their *way of living* changed very little through the years. It is therefore possible to describe their home life and their art without reference to the different periods of ancient Egyptian history.

Of all the early peoples, the Egyptians were the least warlike. Their country was protected by the sea on the north and by deserts to the east and west. For many centuries, they could develop their own way of life without fear of invasion by foreign armies.

Most villages and towns were situated near the **Nile** because it was the chief highway and only source of water. Even the rich lived in mud-brick houses. Windows were small, high openings covered with loosely woven matting to keep out the heat and glare of the sun. The most fashionable district was near the king's palace. Even here, houses were crowded close together to leave more space for farmland. Some dwellings were two stories high. Some opened onto a narrow street; others faced a small walled garden.

The ancient Egyptians stored their water and food in huge *pottery jars.* To prepare foods, the cook used pottery bowls, placing them directly on the fire or in a clay oven. The cook baked bread and cake and roasted beef, mutton, goose, and wildfowl. The common drinks were beer, wine, and milk. Honey and dates were the only sweets.

The members of Egypt's upper classes spent much of their time tending to their appearance. Men shaved with a bronze razor. They cut their hair short and wore wigs. Women also wore wigs or added false braids to their own hair. They had combs and hairpins, and mirrors of polished bronze or silver.

Because of the hot climate, both men and women wore white linen clothes. Men usually wore only a skirt. In the early centuries, the skirts were short and narrow. Later they were long and full. Women wore low-cut white dresses with bands over the shoulders. Both men and women wore jewelry collars and necklaces, strings of beads, bracelets, anklets, earrings, and finger rings. Silver was more precious than gold.

The Lions of AFRICA

by Marna Lee

On the plains of Africa, lions continue to thrive. They do their best hunting on the plateaus of eastern Africa and in the vast grasslands of the south. Their roar is the most fear-inspiring voice of the grasslands. Lions live in rocky dens, in thorn-tree thickets, or in tall grasses at the edges of streams.

Except for the tiger, the lion is the largest member of the cat family. Its body is covered with short yellow-brown hair. A coarse mane grows on the male's head, neck, and shoulders. The female lacks a mane. As a rule, she is more slender and about a foot (30 centimeters) shorter than the male.

Much of the **hunting** is done by the female. Colored like sun-dried grass, the lion can slip unseen across the plains. Its jaws are hinged so that it can open its mouth wide enough to kill a zebra or a medium-sized antelope with one bite.

Lions usually hunt at night. The lion often hides beside a trail leading to a water hole and then pounces upon the shoulder or flank of a passing animal. It drives its claws deep into the flesh and kills its victim with a stabbing and crunching bite on the throat or the back of the neck. When stalking a herd, the lion creeps up from the side toward which the wind is blowing, taking advantage of cover until the moment of the last quick rush.

A *pride* of four to twelve lions sometimes hunts together, working as a team. The **males** roar loudly to scare up the game, while the **females** lie in wait along the trails to pounce on the rushing animals. After the females make a kill, the males come to eat.

Lions usually pair for life. About 16 weeks after mating time, the young (from two to four) are born in a private spot chosen by the mother. She guards her offspring carefully and waits until the cubs are six to eight weeks old before introducing them to the pride. The cubs face danger from predators, as well as unrelated adult males who may kill young cubs in order to bring the lioness into heat again.

Usually lions avoid humans. However, old ones too slow to catch game may become man-eaters. From time to time, a young lion that gets a taste of human blood may continue to kill humans.

Since the days of the Roman Empire, lions have been caged for circuses and zoos. Most of the lions that are seen today in those places have been born in captivity.

ICEBERGS

by Marna Lee

Floating icebergs are at once the dread of sailors and the wonder of all who see them for the first time. They are the broken-off ends of **glaciers** that slide into the sea. Some are small and flat. Others form mountains of ice a mile (1.6 kilometers) or more across and more than 200 feet (61 meters) above the water.

Hiding beneath the sea is the largest part of an iceberg. This part is about seven times as large as the part above. This is because an iceberg is made of *freshwater ice,* which weighs about seven-eighths as much as seawater. In freshwater, an iceberg would sink down until about nine-tenths was below the surface.

These wanderers of the sea are often surrounded by fog. On clear days, they shimmer in the sun with dazzling beauty, reflecting the tints of sea and sky. As they drift, many take on the shapes of castles, arches, and domes. At night, the bergs cause a glow on the bottom of distant clouds called ice blink. Ice blink has been used by sailors to detect the presence of icebergs in the distance.

New icebergs are being formed all the time. Most of those in the **North Atlantic** break off from the fringes of Greenland's great icecap. Here in the early spring thaws, a great parade of floating ice islands begins its journey southward. Sometime in April, May, or June, an average of 400 reach the northern Atlantic shipping routes.

Icebergs melt quickly in salt water. High waves and heavy swells rush the process. As they dissolve, icebergs may split in two, roll over, or slough off great fragments with a vast roar. Some bergs, however, are so huge that they travel 2,000 miles (3,200 kilometers) or more before disappearing.

Two *shipping routes* are especially dangerous: one through the Strait of Belle Isle into the Gulf of St. Lawrence, the other along the Grand Banks. Since 1914, the United States Coast Guard has conducted an ice patrol in the North Atlantic. This service is financed by the maritime nations. Reports of the positions and movements of icebergs are broadcast by radio. The Hydrographic Office issues bulletins that chart the iceberg region. The office also provides charts showing safe "tracks" for shipping. The Coast Guard equips its cutters and planes with radar and loran to fix the location of icebergs. In addition, other sound equipment is lowered into the sea to help locate bergs.

Training Your PUPPY

by Marna Lee

Any young dog can be trained to follow commands and do simple tricks. When correctly trained, a puppy will respond to your commands and gestures. Once you decide to train a puppy, however, you must be willing to stick with the job until the puppy learns.

First, you should select a simple name for the dog. Use the name frequently so that the puppy learns to recognize it.

A training session is best begun when the puppy is hungry because it is more alert at that time. Also, you can reward correct responses with a dog biscuit or meat tidbit. The hungry dog will learn to associate the correct performance of a task with a food reward and be more likely to repeat the task correctly again looking for another reward.

To get the puppy into a collar, entice it to you by extending your open hands. Pat it and say **"good dog"** when it comes. Then slip the collar around its neck. Next, attach a leash to the collar. If the puppy has confidence in you, it will walk along with you even though it is wearing the leash. A metal chain leash is often best because the puppy cannot chew and play with it.

Wait until a puppy is at least six months old before trying to teach it tricks. But do teach it the meaning of **"no"** at an earlier age. Formal training sessions should entail no more than ten minutes of work at a time. They should never tire the dog.

One important command is **"stay."** While the dog is sitting, raise your palm toward the dog and order it to "stay." It will probably try to get up, so tell it "no." Whenever it remains in the sitting position after you have given the command, reward the dog with a tidbit.

More effort might be needed to teach the command "come." When the dog has learned to stay, command it to come and call it by name. When it comes to you, lavish the dog with praise and give it a snack. A stubborn dog might have to be pulled with a cord tied around its collar while the command is given.

If the training sessions are not going well, break them off. Resume them later in the day or even on another day. Give praise and tidbits to the dog only when they are earned.

The Summarization Strategy **39**

Flowering Plants

by Marna Lee

Plants may be classified in a number of ways. A common **classification scheme** organizes plants into groups according to the forms in which they grow. Plants are called *trees* if they have tall, woody stems, or trunks, and are generally 8 feet (2.4 meters) or more in height. *Shrubs* are low, woody plants, usually with many stems branching off close to the ground. *Herbs* have tender, juicy stems in which the woody tissue is much less developed than it is in shrubs and trees.

Flowering plants may be classified according to the length and pattern of their life cycles. **Annuals** complete their life cycle in a single year. The seeds sprout, or germinate, and the seedlings develop into flowering plants. New seeds are produced, and the parent plant dies. All this occurs in a single growing season. Annual plants often grow in habitats that are inhospitable during some part of the year. They survive through these inhospitable periods in the form of seeds, which can withstand environmental extremes. Many familiar garden flowers are annuals, including marigolds, calendulas, zinnias, and nasturtiums.

Biennials require two years to complete their life cycle. In the first year they produce stems and leaves. In the second year they produce blossoms and seeds and then die. During the first year they produce through photosynthesis the food reserves that they need to generate their flowers and seeds the following year. This group also includes many garden flowers, such as Canterbury bells, foxgloves, hollyhocks, and English daisies.

Perennials live for more than two years. The oldest living thing on Earth is thought to be a bristlecone pine that is about 4,900 years old. Many wildflowers are perennial plants. All the common garden perennials, including peonies, irises, and phlox, were developed from wild species. Some perennials produce flowers and seeds throughout their lives. Others, however, produce flowers only once and then die. The American aloe, or century plant, for example, lives for decades while its stem and leaves grow. After 30 to 60 years the plant produces an enormous flowering stalk up to 40 feet (12 meters) tall. Soon after the flowers mature and seeds are produced, the plant dies.

Some perennials are **annual** above ground—that is, their stems, leaves, and blossoms die in the fall. These plants, however, survive through the winter by means of their underground roots and stems. Perennial herbs often grow in this way.

COIN COLLECTING

by Marna Lee

Almost since the first known coins were minted, they have been collected. The art of collecting and studying coins, other currency, and medals is known as numismatics. Some collectors are professionals. They appraise, purchase, and sell coins. But most people collect only as a hobby.

A good coin collection is an **investment** and can be profitable in a number of ways. As a pastime it provides hours of pleasure and the satisfaction of watching the collection grow. Moreover, coins—old, new, foreign, or domestic—will always be worth at least as much as the metals of which they are made. These are often precious metals. The retail value of a coin seldom drops below its face value. A United States cent, for example, will usually be worth at least 1/100 of a United States dollar. The value of many coins can increase over time.

Coins may be of **historical importance** as well. The words and pictures stamped on ancient coins can be the sole source of information about the people who made them. Such coins may bear the only remaining images of famous historical figures or of buildings that have long since disappeared. An old coin is a survival of the past. It brings with it the atmosphere of the age in which it was minted.

The easiest and cheapest way to start collecting is to begin with coins that are still in circulation; everyone carries a certain amount of change. Sorting and saving pennies, nickels, dimes, and quarters helps the beginner start a collection. From this start the collector learns which kinds of coins to acquire. Many beginners buy a coin folder for U.S. 1-cent, 5-cent, or 10-cent pieces and then fill it.

There are many other ways for a beginner to get help in starting a collection. Books about coins and coin collecting can generally be found in public libraries. Coin shops also carry books and catalogs containing valuable information about coins. A beginning collector can find other people who share a similar interest in coins by joining a coin club. *Coin clubs* are a chance for collectors to get together. They exchange information and trade coins. Some clubs hold auctions in which coins are sold to the highest bidder. More than 1,000 local groups have been started all over the United States and Canada.

CLOTHING, A BASIC NEED

by Marna Lee

Like food and shelter, clothing is a basic human need. One reason people began wearing clothing was for *protection.* Rough garments protected them from animal bites, scratches, and burns. Clothing also kept the people warm and dry.

People still wear protective clothing for some types of work and play. The construction worker's hard hat, the chemist's rubber gloves, and the football player's shoulder pads and helmet help protect against injury. The average person may not need special clothing to keep him or her from being hurt. But most people do need warm coats, waterproof overshoes, and sun hats for protection against the weather.

Climate affects the amount and types of clothing that people wear. Those who live in hot, humid African countries may wear very little clothing. If air can flow freely to their skin, perspiration moisture dries more quickly. This helps dispose of body heat.

Many Arabs live in a climate that is hot but dry. Unlike the people of Africa, they wear traditional clothing that covers them from head to toe. Their loose white wool robes reflect the sun's rays and shield them from the hot winds. Such garments also provide insulation against the nighttime cold.

Inuits in Canada and Alaska traditionally wear two layers of clothing, usually sealskin or caribou furs. The inner layer consists of undergarments and socks. The hairy side of undergarments is worn against the skin. Outer garments—trousers, hooded parka, mittens, and boots—are worn with the hairy side out.

PHOTO: Joseph Green/Life File/Getty Images

Copyright © University of Kansas

People who live in mild climates vary their clothing with the seasons. The clothes they wear in summer are usually loosely woven and light in weight. In winter, they may wear extra layers of clothing to hold in the warmth of their bodies. They may also wear a coat of closely woven cloth, leather, or fur to insulate them against the cold.

In recent years, garments have been made to protect people from temperatures more extreme than any encountered on Earth. The space suits worn by the astronauts enable them to function comfortably at widely ranging temperatures, in sunlight or in shade.

Clothing is also worn for reasons other than shelter from heat and cold. One of the most important reasons is **appearance.** People choose clothes that they like and that they think other people will like. They try to select clothes in styles and colors that look good to them and to others.

ANIMAL TRACKS

by Marna Lee

A skilled outdoors person or tracker can tell what creatures have passed through an area from the marks that they have left in the snow, soft earth, mud, or sand. Anyone can make a walk outdoors more interesting by learning to **"read"** the tracks left by animals. Some common animal tracks include tracks of mammals, insects, snakes, and birds.

Snow can be perfect for tracking animals. In winter, animals are very active. Finding food is more difficult at this time. They must roam far and wide in search of something to eat. Fresher tracks show more detail, but smart trackers prefer to wait a night and part of a day after a fresh snowfall. This way both daytime and nighttime feeders have had time to leave their prints.

The **muddy bank of a river** or the edges of a lake may have tracks left by animals that have come to the water to drink. On wet lakeshores and along the marshy shores of ponds, there may be tracks of gulls, sandpipers, and other birds. There may also be footprints of insects, crabs, turtles, and raccoons. A few feet from the sides of a **sandy desert road** may be the tracks of a jackrabbit, a kangaroo rat, or a kit fox. Sand dunes carry the impressions of snakes and insects as well as the tracks of birds and other animals.

A tracker can tell many things from a set of animal tracks. The size of the prints gives a **clue** to the size of the animal. The tracks of the front and back feet may occur in pairs or they may alternate. Some animals walk with their toes pointed inward. Tracks can reveal whether the animal was walking or running. For example, a walking deer places its hind foot directly in the print of the front foot on the same side. When a deer runs, however, its hind feet land in front of the forefoot prints. If it is running very fast, its toes may separate more than usual as its feet hit the ground.

Sometimes tracks tell a dramatic story of flight and pursuit, of capture or escape. The animal may have crouched waiting for some prey. The tracks may suddenly bunch up and then stretch out at the point where the animal spotted its prey and took off in pursuit. Following the trail may reveal whether the animal caught its prey.

Calling All Engineers

by Marna Lee

The building of canals, bridges, and roads was carried out by specially trained civil engineers as early as the middle of the eighteenth century. With the **advent of steam** power at the beginning of the Industrial Revolution in the last part of the eighteenth century, mechanical engineers started to develop engines, locomotives, and various other machines. Originally, steam was used merely to extend power beyond that of animals. During the nineteenth century, however, mechanical engineering expanded to include such laborsaving devices as the sewing machine and the mechanical reaper.

The increasing need for metals furthered mining engineering. With the invention of the Bessemer steel-making process, steel began to replace iron in both machinery and construction. Large bridges and skyscrapers became possible. This led to the development of metallurgical engineering as a separate field. The invention of electric generators and motors and the development of the electric light bulb led to the growth of electrical engineering. This was originally a subspecialty of mechanical engineering. Advances in chemistry during the latter half of the nineteenth century demanded that small-scale laboratories be expanded to large-scale production. This opened the way for the chemical engineer. All these various fields of engineering had been established by 1900.

Following the introduction of the **assembly line** by Henry Ford, the demands of the growing automobile industry led to a specialty in automotive engineering. The rapid spurt of airplane development following World War I led to the new field of aeronautical engineering. The increasing need for **petroleum products** to provide fuels for transportation, energy generation, and heating fostered petroleum engineering. With the development of radio just after the turn of the twentieth century, electronic engineering was born. Radio, television, and almost all modern communications techniques depend on the electronic engineer. Following the invention of the transistor, new vistas in communications and computing were opened. The information revolution caused by the computer added computer engineering as a new specialty.

The advent of nuclear power was reflected in the field of nuclear engineering. Combinations of medicine and technology to build artificial limbs or organs and to improve medical instrumentation started the field of bioengineering.

The need to produce goods cheaply and efficiently became a primary responsibility of the industrial engineer. Following the development of space flight, aerospace engineering was added to aeronautical engineering. A number of further specialty areas also came about such as ceramic, safety, agricultural, environmental, and transportation engineering.

PHOTO: Digital Stock/CORBIS

SWORDFISH

by Marna Lee

Found in tropical and temperate oceans around the world, the swordfish is large and powerful. It grows to about 15 feet (4.6 meters) in length and weighs between 150 and 1,000 pounds (68 to 454 kilograms). Occasionally specimens weighing more than 1,100 pounds (500 kilograms) have been reported.

The swordfish is named for its swordlike jaw extension. This bony, sharp-tipped extension of the upper jaw makes up about one-third of the fish's total length. Because the sword is flattened, rather than rounded as in the marlins and other spear-nosed fishes, it has given rise to a second common name for the swordfish: the **broadbill.**

The swordfish uses its sword to slash through a school of menhaden, herring, mackerel, or squid, killing or stunning its prey, which it then eats at leisure. The sword is also used to fight enemies.

Swordfish eggs are tiny floating globes about 1/16 of an inch (0.16 centimeter) in diameter. They hatch after about two and a half days. The baby swordfish bears little resemblance to the adult. Its body is covered with translucent scales and lined on either side with four rows of spiny plates. The dorsal fin runs the length of the body, and both jaws extend into slender swords of equal length. The baby has sharp teeth. By the time the fish is from 2 to 4 feet (0.6 to 1.2 meters) long, the scales, plates, and teeth disappear. An adult swordfish has no teeth at all. The single dorsal fin of the baby separates into a high, backward-curving lobe and a smaller fin on the tail. The lower jaw shortens and the upper jaw grows to a heavy, saberlike beak.

The Summarization Strategy **49**

The *color* of both young and adult swordfish is gunmetal or bronze above and grayish or silvery below. The fins are dark and leathery. The sword is nearly black on top and paler underneath. Only the eyes of the swordfish are colorful. They are cobalt blue with a narrow rim of pale blue.

Swordfish generally live offshore, occasionally approaching close to the shore to feed. Although they are commonly considered solitary hunters, they sometimes travel or rest in pairs. These fish are often seen resting or swimming near the surface with their dorsal and upper caudal fins protruding above the water. They may descend to great depths, however, in search of food.

The swordfish is a **prized food** and big-game fish.

THE BASICS OF
BICYCLING

by Marna Lee

Bicycling is a simple activity that people of all ages can enjoy. However, pedaling, braking, and shifting gears correctly can improve the fun and efficiency of cycling.

On any bike, **the way a rider pedals** will affect the quality of the ride. The rider should make sure the *bike seat*, or saddle, is properly adjusted. It should be high enough so that the rider's leg is almost fully extended while his or her heel is on the pedal. Toe clips can help make pedal action easier. They allow for a strong downward stroke and an upward thrust.

The best way to achieve smooth, strong pedaling is to practice on low to moderate gears. Most beginners pedal at a rate of only 50 to 60 revolutions per minute (rpm). At 70 to 90 rpm, riders approach peak efficiency and can pedal for hours without strain. Pedaling too long in high gears can cause fatigue and muscle cramps and hurt the knees.

On many bikes, riders *shift gears* to maintain pedaling speed. A typical 10-speed bike has two sizes of chainwheels in front and five gears, or sprockets, in the rear. This combination provides 10 speeds. For flat, open-road riding, a middle gear works best. In middle gear, the chain is on the large chainwheel in front and the middle sprocket in the rear. For climbing hills, a rider should use lower gears in which the chain is on a smaller chainwheel in front and a bigger gear in the rear. For riding downhill or with tailwinds, the rider should shift to a higher gear, which uses the larger chainwheel and a smaller sprocket.

Bicycles have *brakes* for stopping. One-speed bikes have coaster brakes, which a rider operates by pedaling backward. Multispeed bikes have hand brakes. Hand brakes may cause the wheels to lock if their levers are squeezed too hard. A rider should brake by squeezing and then releasing the brake levers in rhythm. On a 10-speed bike, the front wheel supports most of the rider's weight and has the best traction. A rider should use the front brake first. Next, he or she should apply both brakes until the rear wheel locks and then immediately ease the pressure on the rear brake. This will permit that wheel to roll. Then the rider applies the brakes again.

Together, rhythmic braking, proper gear use, and efficient pedaling can make bicycling more enjoyable.

PHOTO: Thinkstock Images/Jupiterimages

Dragons

by Marna Lee

According to a *legend of the Middle Ages,* there once lived in a distant pagan land a dreadful monster called a dragon. The flapping of its great wings could be heard for miles around. With a single blow of its terrible claws it could fell an ox. From the dragon's nostrils came clouds of smoke and flame that brought death to all who breathed it.

Every year a young girl was offered to the dragon to prevent it from rushing upon the city and destroying the inhabitants. One year the lot fell to Princess Sabra, daughter of the king. She was saved by the valiant **St. George,** youngest and bravest of the seven champions of Christendom.

With his magic sword *Ascalon,* he wounded the monster so badly that the princess was able to put her sash about its head and lead it to the marketplace of the town. There St. George slew it with one blow. Won over to the Christian faith by this deed of its champion, the people were baptized.

This is but one of many dragon stories in the folklore of different countries. Before the time of Columbus and the age of discovery, sailors refused to venture into unknown seas for fear of encountering dragons and other monsters of the deep. Old maps show the uncharted seas filled with strange creatures having wings, horns, and claws of such enormous size that they could crush a ship. The dragons of Chinese and Japanese myth and art were reptiles with batlike wings and claws. Such beasts were supposed to spread disease and death among the people.

For ages the dragon was the emblem of the former imperial house of China.

These *superstitions* may have been based on the enormous reptiles that roamed the prehistoric world. Dinosaurs lived in the ages before humans appeared on Earth; however, some reptiles of great size may have existed at the time of the primitive cavemen of Europe. Such creatures could easily have given rise to legends of monsters such as dragons.

In the East Indies certain small lizards—no larger than a human hand—are known as dragons. They are the color of tree bark. The skin along their sides between the legs spreads out into a kind of parachute, enabling them to glide among the branches of the trees in which they live. There are about 20 species of these lizards, all of them harmless.

Have a Prune

by Marna Lee

Certain varieties of **plums** have such firm flesh and high sugar content that they can be dried with little loss of their original plumpness and flavor. These plums are called prune plums, and the dried plums themselves are called prunes.

It is believed that the ancient peoples of the *Middle East* were the first to dry plums to make prunes. Prunes have been prepared for centuries in France, and the prunes from the region around Agen are still considered to be the best in the world. Today, orchards in *California,* which use Agen plums almost exclusively, yield a major share of the world's prunes. Other prune-growing states include Oregon and Washington. Prunes are also produced in some central European and South American countries.

Prune plums are **harvested by machine** or gathered from the ground after they have become so ripe that they can be shaken from the trees. The plums selected for drying are washed in hot water or in a weak lye solution to remove bloom, a powdery coating, and dirt from the skins. Next, they are placed in trays and are dried in the sun or in artificially heated dehydrators. Almost all prunes are dried with the pit intact, though the French Brignolles prune is pitted and peeled before drying. Sun drying may take as long as two weeks; dehydration usually takes no longer than 24 hours. Underdried prunes are removed, and the satisfactory ones are placed in bins for curing for two to three weeks or longer. This process softens the skins hardened by drying and gives the prunes a uniform moisture content.

After curing, the prunes are taken to **packing plants.** Here they are inspected and graded according to size. Large prunes range from 20 to 30 to the pound (0.454 kilograms); there may be as many as 100 smaller

The Summarization Strategy **55**

prunes per pound (0.454 kilogram). Next, the prunes are treated with hot water or steam to sterilize their skins. Finally, they are packed in cardboard cartons or wooden boxes. The choicest are packed like dates and are eaten without cooking.

Prunes are a good source of vitamins A and B; are high in fiber; and are rich in iron, calcium, and phosphorus. Their pulp is used as food for infants. Prunes are eaten raw, soaked or stewed alone or with other fruits, and used in jams and desserts. The pulp, stewed fruit, and juice are packaged commercially.

Acid Rain

by Marna Lee

When **fossil fuels** such as coal, gasoline, and fuel oils are burned, they emit oxides of sulfur, carbon, and nitrogen into the air. These oxides combine with moisture in the air to form sulfuric acid, carbonic acid, and nitric acid. When it rains or snows, these acids fall on Earth in what is called acid rain.

During the twentieth century, the acidity of the air and acid rain have come to be recognized as leading threats to the stability and quality of Earth's environment. Most of this acidity is produced in the industrialized nations of the Northern Hemisphere—the United States, Canada, Japan, and many countries of Europe. The **effects of acid rain** can be devastating to many forms of life, including human life. Its effects can be most vividly seen, however, in lakes, rivers, and streams. Acidity in water kills virtually all life forms. By the early 1990s, tens of thousands of lakes had been destroyed by acid rain. The problem has been most severe in Norway, Sweden, and Canada.

Scientists use what is called the *pH factor* to measure the acidity or alkalinity of liquid solutions. On a scale from 0 to 14, the number 0 represents the highest level of acid. Fourteen represents the most basic or alkaline. Rainfalls in the eastern United States and in Western Europe often have a pH factor ranging from 4.5 to 4.0.

The threat posed by acid rain is not limited by geographic boundaries. Prevailing winds carry the pollutants around the globe. For example, much research supports the conclusion that pollution from coal-powered electric generating stations in the midwestern United States is the ultimate cause of the severe acid-rain problem in eastern Canada and the northeastern United States. Nor are the **destructive effects** of acid rain limited to the natural environment. Structures made

The Summarization Strategy **57**

of stone, metal, and cement have also been damaged or destroyed. Some of the world's greatest monuments have shown signs of deterioration. This deterioration is probably caused by acid rain.

The cost of antipollution equipment such as burners, filters, and chemical and washing devices is great. However, the cost in damage to the environment and human life is estimated to be much greater because the damage caused by acid rain may be irreversible. Although preventive measures are being taken, up to 500,000 lakes in North America may be destroyed before the end of the twentieth century.

Comprehension Tests

Name: _____   Date: _____

Leaving a Fire ⚠️

_____ 1. The time to plan for a fire emergency is
   a. before one happens.
   b. during the emergency.
   c. after an emergency happens.

_____ 2. The best way out of the building in a fire is
   a. a window.
   b. jumping from the roof.
   c. the route you use every day.

_____ 3. The key to a safe escape from a fire is
   a. practice.
   b. early warning.
   c. the fire department.

_____ 4. It is a good idea to practice an escape plan
   a. when it is dark.
   b. every day.
   c. early in the morning.

_____ 5. After escaping from a fire, you should
   a. gather at an agreed-upon place.
   b. call an ambulance.
   c. run back into the building.

_____ 6. You can conclude from the article that in a fire emergency,
   a. it is important to move slowly.
   b. every second counts.
   c. everyone needs help.

_____ 7. It is likely that people involved in a fire emergency will be
   a. cowardly.
   b. panicky.
   c. calm.

_____ 8. It is important to plan a variety of escape routes because
   a. plans should be complicated.
   b. it is easy to get lost in a fire.
   c. one or more routes may be blocked by fire.

_____ 9. You can conclude that the longer a family takes to escape, the
   a. more damage a fire will cause.
   b. more likely they are to escape safely.
   c. less likely they are to escape safely.

_____ 10. You can conclude that escape from fire is
   a. highly unlikely.
   b. impossible unless a plan is followed.
   c. possible.

SCORE: _____ /10

Name: _____   Date: _____

Backpacking

____ 1. When packing for a hike, backpackers try to
   a. add ounces.
   b. stock extra supplies.
   c. save weight.

____ 2. The most popular shoes for all-around hiking are made of
   a. rubber.
   b. light fabric.
   c. leather.

____ 3. Hikers should wear
   a. new boots.
   b. comfortable boots.
   c. boots with leather soles.

____ 4. In the wilderness, most hiking trails
   a. are unmarked.
   b. follow natural streams.
   c. are well marked.

____ 5. Mistakes in plans should be corrected
   a. on a map.
   b. after a trial run.
   c. during a long hike.

____ 6. Backpackers should most likely plan on
   a. bringing their own sleeping shelters.
   b. sleeping outside.
   c. sleeping in cabins along the way.

____ 7. The article suggests that backpacking
   a. can be dangerous.
   b. is challenging.
   c. requires little planning.

____ 8. Backpacking is probably not an activity for
   a. youngsters.
   b. people who like adventure.
   c. people who are out of shape.

____ 9. You can conclude from the article that it is important for backpackers to
   a. wear the proper clothing.
   b. wear several layers of clothing.
   c. carry a heavy jacket.

____ 10. When hiking in the wilderness, you should have the goal to
   a. break in new shoes.
   b. enjoy the freedom of wilderness travel.
   c. follow marked trails.

SCORE: _____ /10

Name: _____   Date: _____

A Family of PLANETS

_____ 1. The sun's family includes
   a. seven planets.
   b. eight planets.
   c. nine planets.

_____ 2. In the night sky, planets shine
   a. with their own light.
   b. because of the moonlight.
   c. with reflected light.

_____ 3. A planet that was discovered after the invention of the telescope is
   a. Venus.
   b. Jupiter.
   c. Neptune.

_____ 4. Planets stay in their orbits around the sun because of
   a. reflection.
   b. gravity.
   c. secondhand sunlight.

_____ 5. Each planet moves with a speed that
   a. just balances the sun's pull.
   b. changes daily.
   c. varies with the seasons.

_____ 6. You can conclude from the article that the planets that can be seen with the naked eye move
   a. faster than those that cannot.
   b. slower than those that cannot.
   c. both faster and slower than those that cannot.

_____ 7. You can conclude that compared to a star, a planet is
   a. hotter.
   b. cooler.
   c. about the same temperature.

_____ 8. The article suggests that studying the skies
   a. is no longer useful.
   b. began with the invention of the telescope.
   c. is an ancient pastime.

_____ 9. You can conclude that if the planets were to reduce their speed, they would
   a. be pulled into the sun.
   b. fall into the universe.
   c. bump into each other.

_____ 10. You can conclude that without the sun's light, Earth would
   a. receive light from the moon.
   b. not exist.
   c. be cold and dark.

SCORE: _____ /10

Name: _____   Date: _____

Alfred the Great

____ 1. During Alfred's time, England
    a. was Europe's leading nation.
    b. consisted of four small kingdoms.
    c. was never invaded.

____ 2. Alfred fought against
    a. Saxon kings.
    b. German traders.
    c. Danish invaders.

____ 3. Alfred was forced to go into hiding
    a. after a military defeat.
    b. to recover his health.
    c. when his brother died.

____ 4. Alfred was known as a warrior and a
    a. businessperson.
    b. scientist.
    c. political leader.

____ 5. After Alfred's death, England was
    a. ruled by his son.
    b. divided up again.
    c. overrun by the Danes.

____ 6. According to the article, Alfred was
    a. physically strong but not too intelligent.
    b. an admirable leader of his people.
    c. a true king of England.

____ 7. Alfred cannot be compared to the kings who followed him because he
    a. did not rule the whole country.
    b. was never really proclaimed king.
    c. was more a warrior than a king.

____ 8. It is likely that without Alfred's leadership,
    a. the Saxons would have been defeated by the Danes.
    b. the Saxons would have defeated the Danes.
    c. the English language would have disappeared.

____ 9. A word that might be used to describe Alfred is
    a. deceptive.
    b. temperamental.
    c. dynamic.

____ 10. If Alfred were alive today, he would most likely be a
    a. king.
    b. soldier.
    c. lawyer or a teacher.

SCORE: _____ /10

Comprehension Test

Name: _____   Date: _____

ᴡᴡ Tracking the Emperor Goose ᴡᴡ

_____ 1. The Emperor Goose is found in
   a. Australia.
   b. South America.
   c. North America.

_____ 2. To study the birds, scientists
   a. read books about them.
   b. set up camps near the breeding grounds.
   c. place them in zoos.

_____ 3. After the Emperor Geese mate,
   a. the male flies away.
   b. the female wanders off.
   c. they stay together.

_____ 4. Goslings take on a blue tone
   a. when they get cold.
   b. after they hatch.
   c. when they reach the fledgling stage.

_____ 5. The head of the adult goose
   a. makes it very colorful.
   b. is white in color.
   c. matches its yellow-orange feet.

_____ 6. The article suggests that the Emperor Goose
   a. is threatened by pollution.
   b. will soon become extinct.
   c. is too rare to survive.

_____ 7. You can conclude from the article that Emperor Geese prefer a
   a. warm climate.
   b. cool climate.
   c. stormy environment.

_____ 8. You can conclude that the Emperor Goose protects its nest by
   a. resembling its surroundings.
   b. choosing small nesting sites.
   c. changing colors.

_____ 9. Probably the best way to study a wild creature is to
   a. capture it.
   b. look at photographs.
   c. enter its habitat.

_____ 10. You can conclude that the more that is learned about the Emperor Goose,
   a. the more likely it is to survive.
   b. the faster it will multiply.
   c. the more geese scientists can find.

SCORE: _____ /10

Name: _____   Date: _____

Building the Pyramids

_____ 1. Pyramids were built as
   a. houses for the wealthy.
   b. burial places.
   c. warehouses.

_____ 2. Pyramids were built on the west bank of the Nile because the
   a. ground was softer there.
   b. sun rose in that direction.
   c. sun set in that direction.

_____ 3. For building the pyramids, farmers received
   a. high wages.
   b. food and clothing.
   c. gold.

_____ 4. Stones from the desert were brought to the building site
   a. on wheeled carts.
   b. on sleds with wide wooden runners.
   c. by boat.

_____ 5. Tools used to build the pyramids were made of
   a. iron.
   b. strong wood.
   c. flint or copper.

_____ 6. Farmers worked on the pyramids when the Nile river was low, which suggests that the river
   a. provided water for growing crops.
   b. frequently dried up.
   c. was the only source of water in Egypt.

_____ 7. You can conclude from the article that building a pyramid
   a. was a year-round job.
   b. was done solely by farmers.
   c. took many years.

_____ 8. According to the article, the Egyptians were
   a. clever engineers.
   b. good farmers.
   c. talented artists.

_____ 9. The article suggests that building the pyramids was
   a. very difficult.
   b. easy work.
   c. wasteful.

_____ 10. You can conclude from the article that Egyptian kings wanted
   a. small, simple tombs.
   b. to be forgotten after they died.
   c. to be remembered after they died.

SCORE: _____ /10

Copyright © University of Kansas

Comprehension Test

Name: _____   Date: _____

COLORS

_____ 1. Color cannot exist apart from
  a. shape.
  b. the sun.
  c. light.

_____ 2. Color can indicate whether a plant
  a. has shape.
  b. is sick.
  c. bears fruit.

_____ 3. White light is
  a. the absence of color.
  b. a mixture of many different colors.
  c. a mixture of three colors.

_____ 4. A rainbow-like band of different colors is called
  a. the visible spectrum.
  b. a prism.
  c. reflected light.

_____ 5. The seventeenth-century scientist who experimented with light was
  a. Richard Isaac.
  b. Isaac Newton.
  c. Thomas Edison.

_____ 6. Without color, the visible world would be
  a. invisible.
  b. less interesting.
  c. shapeless.

_____ 7. You can conclude from the article that before Newton's experiments, white light was thought to be
  a. prismatic.
  b. blue.
  c. white.

_____ 8. You can conclude from the article that light
  a. gives objects their shape.
  b. gives objects their color.
  c. determines the size of an object.

_____ 9. In the dark, an orange carrot would be
  a. orange.
  b. black.
  c. colorless.

_____ 10. The rainbow that sometimes appears after a storm is the result of sunlight aimed at water droplets, which suggests that water droplets act as a
  a. prism.
  b. visible spectrum.
  c. microscope.

SCORE: _____ /10

Name: _____   Date: _____

Machines for TRANSPORTATION

_____ 1. The first sources of transportation were
   a. boats.
   b. animals.
   c. carts.

_____ 2. The invention of the wheel made it possible to
   a. move larger loads.
   b. eliminate pack animals.
   c. harness the wind.

_____ 3. Nineteenth-century clipper ships depended on
   a. steam power.
   b. wind power.
   c. gas power.

_____ 4. George Stephenson invented a
   a. steamboat.
   b. steam locomotive.
   c. gas engine.

_____ 5. A fuel not used by ocean steamers was
   a. wood.
   b. coal.
   c. gas.

_____ 6. You can conclude from the article that the biggest influence on transportation has been
   a. animals.
   b. machines.
   c. the steam engine.

_____ 7. From the article, you can conclude that wind power is
   a. an efficient source of power.
   b. an unreliable source of power.
   c. no longer used as a source of power.

_____ 8. A secondary power source for paddle-wheel ocean steamers was
   a. water.
   b. gas.
   c. wind.

_____ 9. The article suggests that transportation is
   a. necessary to the modern way of life.
   b. a necessary evil.
   c. more a luxury than a necessity.

_____ 10. It is likely that the transportation industry
   a. will benefit from new inventions.
   b. has reached its limits.
   c. will emphasize the past rather than the future.

SCORE: _____ /10

Name: _____ Date: _____

A Pet Parakeet

_____ 1. Budgie is another name for a
   a. parrot.
   b. parakeet.
   c. mature bird.

_____ 2. When you bring your parakeet home, at first you should
   a. finger-train it.
   b. let it explore your home.
   c. let it stay in its cage.

_____ 3. A parakeet should be fed
   a. once a day.
   b. twice a day.
   c. three times a day.

_____ 4. You can teach your bird to talk
   a. when it is mature.
   b. as soon as it is cage-tame.
   c. as soon as you bring it home.

_____ 5. Parakeets easily learn words starting with
   a. *s* and *t*.
   b. *b* and *c*.
   c. *p* and *b*.

_____ 6. The article suggests that parakeets make
   a. interesting pets.
   b. poor pets.
   c. dangerous pets.

_____ 7. You can conclude from the article that parakeets like
   a. a varied diet.
   b. the same food every day.
   c. the same food that people eat.

_____ 8. You can conclude that it is best to train a parakeet
   a. all at once.
   b. once a week.
   c. in stages.

_____ 9. Parakeets probably learn to talk by
   a. reading lips.
   b. imitating sounds.
   c. making up sounds.

_____ 10. You can conclude that a parakeet learns faster when it
   a. is rewarded with food.
   b. can learn from other birds.
   c. is not distracted.

SCORE: _____ /10

Name: _____   Date: _____

People's BEST Friend

____ 1. The dog is called a person's best friend because of its
    a. loyalty to a master.
    b. ability to save lives.
    c. friendly nature.

____ 2. The wild ancestors of dogs were
    a. herders.
    b. hunters.
    c. cave dwellers.

____ 3. Dogs prefer
    a. living alone.
    b. being with a pack.
    c. living indoors.

____ 4. Dogs that make good watchdogs include
    a. beagles.
    b. Welsh corgis.
    c. German shepherds.

____ 5. A dog with many breeds in its background is called a
    a. purebred.
    b. range animal.
    c. mongrel.

____ 6. Dogs are popular pets because
    a. of their loyalty and affectionate nature.
    b. of their great variety.
    c. they once were hunters.

____ 7. You can conclude from the article that the temperament of a mongrel dog is
    a. easy to predict.
    b. difficult to predict.
    c. usually aggressive.

____ 8. A dog that is attacked will most likely
    a. wag its tail.
    b. bite to defend itself.
    c. tuck its tail between its legs.

____ 9. Dogs that were bred for hunting
    a. may make good family pets.
    b. seldom make good family pets.
    c. are usually aggressive animals.

____ 10. You can conclude from the article that people choose as pets those dogs that
    a. best suit their needs.
    b. easily fit into family life.
    c. make good watchdogs.

SCORE: _____ /10

Name: _____   Date: _____

A Desert Fox

_____ 1. In size, a kit fox resembles a
   a. large house cat.
   b. kangaroo rat.
   c. pocket mouse.

_____ 2. To a kit fox, people are
   a. frightening.
   b. objects of curiosity.
   c. natural enemies.

_____ 3. A kit fox's diet consists mostly of
   a. plants.
   b. insects.
   c. small animals.

_____ 4. A desert hunter's most important sense is
   a. sight.
   b. hearing.
   c. smell.

_____ 5. A distinctive characteristic of the kit fox is its
   a. ears.
   b. nose.
   c. head.

_____ 6. You can conclude from the article that the kit fox is
   a. smaller than other foxes.
   b. larger than other foxes.
   c. about the same size as other foxes.

_____ 7. It is likely that the kit fox
   a. will learn to fear people.
   b. has not been harmed by people.
   c. will learn to trust people.

_____ 8. You can conclude that adaptations made by animals
   a. are more pronounced in the desert.
   b. vary according to where they live.
   c. are usually changes in coloring.

_____ 9. It is likely that a kit fox's shyness
   a. helps it find food.
   b. allows it to hear better.
   c. protects it from its enemies.

_____ 10. You can conclude that a kit fox does most of its hunting
   a. at night.
   b. during the afternoon.
   c. in the morning.

SCORE: _____ /10

Name: _____   Date: _____

BUILDING A 10-SPEED

_____ 1. The price of a 10-speed bicycle
   a. is the same everywhere.
   b. varies with the quality of the parts.
   c. is determined by its size.

_____ 2. A custom-built 10-speed is built according to
   a. wheel size.
   b. who will use it and how it will be used.
   c. conventional standards.

_____ 3. Quality 10-speed bikes are often made of
   a. tin.
   b. nickel plating.
   c. high-carbon steel.

_____ 4. Brazing is a method of
   a. weakening metal.
   b. holding metal together.
   c. cleaning frames.

_____ 5. The final coat of paint on a quality bicycle is
   a. the top coat.
   b. the primer.
   c. lacquer.

_____ 6. From the article you can conclude that custom-built bikes
   a. cost less than conventional bikes.
   b. are more expensive than conventional bikes.
   c. cost the same as conventional bikes.

_____ 7. A bike racer would prefer a bicycle that
   a. provides maximum speed for every ounce of energy the rider uses.
   b. requires the most energy from the rider.
   c. has the least weight and the largest wheels.

_____ 8. From the article you can conclude that the best racing bicycles are
   a. painted red.
   b. light in weight.
   c. made of plastic.

_____ 9. From the article you can conclude that the most popular bicycles in the United States are
   a. 2-speeds.
   b. 5-speeds.
   c. 10-speeds.

_____ 10. Most cyclists in the United States ride
   a. custom-built bikes.
   b. conventional bikes.
   c. unicycles.

SCORE: _____ /10

Name: _____   Date: _____

The Florida Keys

_____ 1. The Florida Keys include
   a. 60 keys from Miami Beach to Key West.
   b. 100 keys from Miami Beach to Cuba.
   c. 50 keys from Ft. Lauderdale to Miami Beach.

_____ 2. The largest of the keys is
   a. Key West.
   b. Key Largo.
   c. Miami Beach.

_____ 3. Settlers in Key West in the sixteenth century included the
   a. Spanish.
   b. Dutch.
   c. Portuguese.

_____ 4. A current problem in the Florida Keys is
   a. lack of salt water.
   b. a food shortage.
   c. lack of fresh water.

_____ 5. A major industry in Key West is
   a. tourism.
   b. hunting.
   c. airplane construction.

_____ 6. You can conclude from the article that a major tourist attraction in the Florida Keys is
   a. a colorful past.
   b. good weather.
   c. Cuban cigars.

_____ 7. You can conclude from the article that the smallest keys are
   a. the most crowded.
   b. uninhabited.
   c. wildlife sanctuaries.

_____ 8. It is likely that most of the food in the Florida Keys is
   a. imported.
   b. grown in green houses.
   c. exported.

_____ 9. The water problem in the keys is most likely due to
   a. industrial pollution.
   b. an overabundance of salt water.
   c. their distance from the mainland.

_____ 10. Without the tourist trade, the economy of the keys would probably rely mainly on
   a. government funding.
   b. construction.
   c. commercial fishing.

SCORE: _____ /10

Name: _____   Date: _____

THE AMOEBA

_____ 1. The substance that makes up all living things is called
  a. amoeba.
  b. bacteria.
  c. protoplasm.

_____ 2. The body of an amoeba is composed of one
  a. membrane.
  b. cell.
  c. pseudopod.

_____ 3. The activities of an amoeba are controlled by a
  a. cytoplasm.
  b. membrane.
  c. nucleus.

_____ 4. An amoeba reproduces by
  a. producing an egg.
  b. dividing in half.
  c. dividing into three parts.

_____ 5. The environment of an amoeba
  a. has no effect on the amoeba.
  b. causes the amoeba to react.
  c. makes it reproduce.

_____ 6. Pseudopods enable the amoeba to
  a. travel and feed.
  b. divide and reproduce.
  c. take in and release water.

_____ 7. The protective membrane of an amoeba can be compared to
  a. human skin.
  b. a rubber ball.
  c. a tree root.

_____ 8. Without its flexible membrane an amoeba would be likely to
  a. fill itself with bubbles.
  b. starve.
  c. change shape.

_____ 9. The nucleus of an amoeba functions as a kind of
  a. mouth.
  b. brain.
  c. arm.

_____ 10. From the article you can conclude that after an amoeba divides,
  a. each half will eventually reproduce.
  b. the nucleus dies.
  c. one half will grow larger than the other.

SCORE: _____ /10

Name: _____   Date: _____

Take a Deep Breath

_____ 1. No one can live for more than a few days without
   a. breathing.
   b. food.
   c. water.

_____ 2. Humans usually breathe about
   a. 18 times a minute.
   b. 25 times a minute.
   c. 10 times a minute.

_____ 3. Air is made up mostly of
   a. oxygen.
   b. carbon dioxide.
   c. nitrogen.

_____ 4. To produce energy, cells need
   a. carbon dioxide.
   b. nitrogen.
   c. oxygen.

_____ 5. A waste product of cells using oxygen is
   a. nitrogen.
   b. carbon dioxide.
   c. water vapor.

_____ 6. You can conclude from the article that the most vital element to life is
   a. water.
   b. food.
   c. air.

_____ 7. It is likely that compared to a body in motion, a body at rest
   a. uses less energy.
   b. uses more energy.
   c. is using more carbon dioxide.

_____ 8. You can conclude from the article that gasping for breath indicates that the body
   a. needs more oxygen.
   b. needs less oxygen.
   c. is using more carbon dioxide.

_____ 9. The article suggests that rare gases
   a. play an important role in breathing.
   b. are probably unimportant to breathing.
   c. are a by-product of breathing.

_____ 10. You can conclude from the article that as you breathe, the balance of gases
   a. always stays the same.
   b. varies according to circumstances.
   c. depends mainly on where you are.

SCORE: _____ /10

Name: _____   Date: _____

FLAX

_____ 1. Linen is made from
   a. the linen plant.
   b. animal hides.
   c. the flax plant.

_____ 2. The process of rotting flax is called
   a. scotching.
   b. drying.
   c. retting.

_____ 3. The United States does not grow much flax because
   a. growing conditions are poor in the United States.
   b. imported flax is cheaper.
   c. harvesting it is too difficult.

_____ 4. Seed from flax is used in
   a. cigarettes.
   b. rugs.
   c. paints.

_____ 5. Fiber flax plants are pulled up by the roots because
   a. the roots are a useful byproduct.
   b. cutting injures the fibers.
   c. pulling is easier than cutting.

_____ 6. If a fiber flax plant becomes woody, the plant may have
   a. received insufficient rain.
   b. endured a short, cool growing season.
   c. been pulled up too soon.

_____ 7. In processing linen, bacteria are
   a. useless.
   b. indispensable.
   c. dangerous.

_____ 8. The characteristics of linen cloth make it desirable for making
   a. tablecloths.
   b. veils.
   c. lace.

_____ 9. From the article you can conclude that the flax plant is raised primarily for its
   a. beauty.
   b. usefulness.
   c. food value.

_____ 10. Ancient Egyptian mummies were wrapped in linen, which suggests that
   a. linen was the only cloth known at the time.
   b. Egyptians were the first to make cloth.
   c. Egyptians recognized the durability of linen.

SCORE: _____ /10

Name: _____   Date: _____

Everyday Life in ANCIENT EGYPT

_____ 1. The Egyptians were most creative
   a. at the beginning of their history.
   b. during the middle years of their history.
   c. at the end of their history.

_____ 2. Egypt is bordered on three sides by
   a. water.
   b. desert.
   c. the sea and deserts.

_____ 3. The only source of water for Egyptians was
   a. the sea.
   b. underground wells.
   c. the Nile.

_____ 4. The most valued metal for jewelry in ancient Egypt was
   a. silver.
   b. gold.
   c. bronze.

_____ 5. Cooking utensils were made of
   a. metal.
   b. stone.
   c. pottery.

_____ 6. Regarding their appearance, upper-class Egyptians could be considered
   a. vain.
   b. modest.
   c. casual.

_____ 7. You can conclude from the article that the Nile was
   a. a large, paved road.
   b. an inland waterway.
   c. Egypt's only street.

_____ 8. It is likely that the Egyptians' lifestyle changed very little because of
   a. a lack of foreign influence.
   b. the hot weather.
   c. boredom.

_____ 9. Silver was more precious than gold probably because it was
   a. easier to find.
   b. scarcer.
   c. easier to shape.

_____ 10. The Egyptians' concern for personal appearance is suggested by their wearing of
   a. white linen.
   b. skirts.
   c. jewelry.

SCORE: _____ /10

Name: _____   Date: _____

The Lions of AFRICA

_____ 1. Compared to other members of the cat family, the lion is
  a. small.
  b. the largest.
  c. the second largest.

_____ 2. Lions usually hunt
  a. at sunrise.
  b. during the day.
  c. at night.

_____ 3. A group of lions is called a
  a. herd.
  b. pride.
  c. flock.

_____ 4. Young lions are in danger from
  a. the mother lion.
  b. unrelated adult males.
  c. other cubs.

_____ 5. Most lions seen in zoos today are born in
  a. captivity.
  b. Africa.
  c. the wild.

_____ 6. You can conclude from the article that a lion's coloring
  a. changes with the seasons.
  b. varies according to where it lives.
  c. helps it hide from its prey.

_____ 7. It is likely that lions stalk their prey against the wind in order to
  a. reduce the sound of their approach.
  b. keep their scent from carrying.
  c. keep cooler.

_____ 8. You can conclude that lions are
  a. feared by most other animals.
  b. ignored by most other animals.
  c. protected by most other animals.

_____ 9. You can conclude that lions usually avoid humans because people
  a. are the enemies of lions.
  b. are difficult to stalk.
  c. are harder to hunt than herd animals.

_____ 10. Throughout history, humans have regarded lions as
  a. pets.
  b. fascinating creatures.
  c. terrifying enemies.

SCORE: _____ /10

Name: _____   **Date:** _____

ICEBERGS

____ 1. Floating icebergs are
   a. mountains of frozen salt water.
   b. broken-off ends of glaciers.
   c. flat chunks of frozen snow.

____ 2. The ratio of an iceberg's parts that are below to those that are above the water is about
   a. two to one.
   b. seven to one.
   c. twenty to one.

____ 3. The word *ice blink* refers to
   a. the southward journey of icebergs.
   b. an iceberg's shape.
   c. a white glow on a cloud indicating the presence of an iceberg.

____ 4. Icebergs floating in seawater
   a. grow in size.
   b. quickly sink.
   c. quickly melt.

____ 5. The locations of icebergs are charted using
   a. fishing nets.
   b. radar and loran.
   c. weather balloons.

____ 6. You can conclude from the article that freshwater
   a. is less buoyant than salt water.
   b. is more buoyant than salt water.
   c. has about the same buoyancy as salt water.

____ 7. You can conclude that icebergs present a danger to
   a. anything in their path.
   b. wildlife.
   c. airplanes.

____ 8. The Coast Guard's aim in charting icebergs is to
   a. control their course.
   b. speed up the melting process.
   c. prevent collisions.

____ 9. You can conclude that fixing the location of an iceberg
   a. is an ongoing process.
   b. prevents it from moving further.
   c. is a simple task.

____ 10. It is likely that before the use of modern technology to track icebergs,
   a. collisions were a constant danger.
   b. ships avoided the North Atlantic.
   c. there were few collisions.

SCORE: _____ /10

Name: _____   Date: _____

Training Your PUPPY

_____ 1. The first step in training a puppy is to
   a. feed the puppy.
   b. name the puppy.
   c. collar the puppy.

_____ 2. A puppy should be trained when it
   a. is hungry.
   b. is six months old.
   c. has just been fed.

_____ 3. Formal training sessions should be limited to
   a. no more than ten minutes of work at a time.
   b. half an hour, once a week.
   c. two times a day.

_____ 4. When a dog performs properly, it should be
   a. allowed to rest.
   b. rewarded with food.
   c. commanded to sit.

_____ 5. If training sessions are not going well, a trainer should
   a. punish the puppy.
   b. wait until the puppy is older.
   c. temporarily break off training.

_____ 6. The article suggests that dogs should be taught commands
   a. in order of difficulty.
   b. in whatever way an owner chooses.
   c. only in the morning.

_____ 7. Good training requires a
   a. smart dog.
   b. dedicated owner.
   c. strong leash.

_____ 8. It is likely that puppies are better able to remember names that are
   a. spoken loudly.
   b. short and simple.
   c. long and complicated.

_____ 9. You can conclude from the article that dogs learn best when they are rewarded
   a. at the beginning of each training session.
   b. at the end of each training session.
   c. for performing correctly.

_____ 10. You can conclude from the article that dogs learn faster when
   a. they have confidence in the trainer.
   b. they are well fed.
   c. trainers show affection.

SCORE: _____ /10

Name: _____   Date: _____

Flowering Plants

_____ 1. One way to organize plants is by
  a. how quickly they grow.
  b. when they flower.
  c. the forms in which they grow.

_____ 2. Flowering plants called annuals
  a. die after a year.
  b. bloom once a year for 10 years.
  c. thrive in difficult climates.

_____ 3. Biennials complete their life cycles in
  a. half a year.
  b. two years.
  c. two weeks.

_____ 4. The oldest living thing on Earth is about
  a. 500 years old.
  b. 5,000 years old.
  c. 25,000 years old.

_____ 5. Perennial plants live
  a. for more than two years.
  b. about five years.
  c. forever.

_____ 6. From the article you can conclude that many plants survive by
  a. adapting to their environments.
  b. migrating.
  c. producing flowers.

_____ 7. The stage at which a plant most likely endures a harsh environment is the
  a. seed.
  b. seedling.
  c. mature plant.

_____ 8. From the article you can conclude that the various classification schemes for plants are
  a. continually changing.
  b. based on different characteristics.
  c. not scientifically organized.

_____ 9. A gardener who wants a different garden every year should plant mostly
  a. annuals.
  b. biennials.
  c. perennials.

_____ 10. The best time to plant a seedling outdoors is
  a. during warm weather.
  b. when the flowers mature.
  c. after they become shrubs.

SCORE: _____ /10

Name: _____   Date: _____

COIN COLLECTING

_____ 1. The art of collecting coins is known as
  a. numismatics.
  b. mathematics.
  c. metallurgy.

_____ 2. The retail value of a coin is usually
  a. more than its face value.
  b. its face value.
  c. the cost of its metal.

_____ 3. The easiest way to begin a coin collection is with
  a. rare, old coins.
  b. fifty-cent pieces.
  c. coins in circulation.

_____ 4. A penny is worth at least
  a. 1/10 of a United States dollar.
  b. 2 cents.
  c. 1/100 of a United States dollar.

_____ 5. Coin collection can be profitable because all coins
  a. increase in value.
  b. are always worth at least as much as the metals of which they are made.
  c. bear images of famous people.

_____ 6. If the demand for a coin decreases while the supply increases, the coin will most likely
  a. retain its value.
  b. increase in value.
  c. drop in value.

_____ 7. Coin collectors are most likely
  a. impatient.
  b. curious.
  c. mechanical.

_____ 8. Numismatics is a hobby that requires
  a. training.
  b. wealth.
  c. an interest in coins.

_____ 9. From the article you can conclude that coin collecting is
  a. a popular hobby.
  b. an unusual hobby.
  c. limited to professionals.

_____ 10. A benefit of coin collection is that it
  a. can be profitable.
  b. helps preserve rare coins.
  c. forces saving.

SCORE: _____ / 10

Name: _____   Date: _____

CLOTHING, A BASIC NEED

_____ 1. People began wearing clothing for
   a. decoration.
   b. protection.
   c. amusement.

_____ 2. The amount and types of clothing people wear are affected by
   a. air pollution.
   b. work habits.
   c. climate.

_____ 3. The loose, white wool robes worn by Arabs help
   a. reflect the sun's rays.
   b. allow hot winds to flow through.
   c. provide warmth during cool summers.

_____ 4. Inuit clothing usually consists of
   a. wool.
   b. animal skins or furs.
   c. cotton.

_____ 5. To help keep warm during cold winter months, people wear
   a. loosely knit clothing.
   b. lightweight clothing.
   c. layers of clothing.

_____ 6. If moisture from perspiration dries quickly, body temperature is likely to
   a. drop.
   b. rise.
   c. stay the same.

_____ 7. In hot, humid climates, people are likely to wear
   a. more clothing.
   b. less clothing.
   c. tight clothing.

_____ 8. Based on what you know about white clothing, you would expect darker clothing to
   a. retain moisture.
   b. reflect heat.
   c. absorb heat.

_____ 9. You can conclude from the article that how people appear to others is
   a. not important to most people.
   b. a concern to most people.
   c. has little to do with clothing.

_____ 10. Clothing made for astronauts must be
   a. adaptable.
   b. cool.
   c. heavy.

Copyright © University of Kansas

SCORE: _____ /10

Name: _____   Date: _____

ANIMAL TRACKS

_____ 1. Trackers are
   a. creatures passing through an area.
   b. people who read marks left by animals.
   c. prints left by animals.

_____ 2. The size of prints left by an animal tells
   a. the size of the animal.
   b. when the animal passed through an area.
   c. the animal's sex.

_____ 3. Animal tracks can reveal
   a. an animal's thoughts.
   b. whether an animal was running.
   c. the color of an animal.

_____ 4. Trackers prefer to read prints
   a. right after a snowfall.
   b. during a snowfall.
   c. a night and part of a day after a snowfall.

_____ 5. Animals are very active in winter because
   a. they must roam farther in search of food.
   b. they must move to keep warm.
   c. cold weather makes them hungrier.

_____ 6. The article wants you to understand that animal tracks
   a. all look alike.
   b. are easy to read.
   c. are different for each animal.

_____ 7. You can conclude from the article that frozen earth
   a. is good for tracking animals.
   b. is the best surface for tracking animals.
   c. makes tracking difficult.

_____ 8. Snow is perfect for tracking animals because
   a. details are clearer on a soft surface.
   b. animals like walking on snow.
   c. snow melts quickly.

_____ 9. Trackers are likely to be
   a. studious.
   b. curious.
   c. greedy.

_____ 10. You can conclude from the article that hunters read animal tracks in order to
   a. locate their prey.
   b. avoid dangerous wild animals.
   c. predict the weather.

SCORE: _____ /10

Name: _____   Date: _____

Calling All Engineers

____ 1. Steam power was introduced at the beginning of
   a. the Industrial Revolution.
   b. World War II.
   c. the Revolutionary War.

____ 2. Iron in machinery and construction was replaced by
   a. aluminum.
   b. ceramics.
   c. steel.

____ 3. Electronic engineering was fostered by the development of
   a. the sewing machine.
   b. the radio.
   c. television.

____ 4. Among other things, bioengineering involves building
   a. nuclear power stations.
   b. airplanes.
   c. artificial limbs and organs.

____ 5. Industrial engineers are concerned with
   a. improving medical instrumentation.
   b. producing goods cheaply and efficiently.
   c. developing new areas of communication.

____ 6. You can conclude from the article that engineering
   a. is a broad field with many specialty areas.
   b. is restricted to industrial applications.
   c. specializes in aeronautical applications.

____ 7. Engineers are concerned with
   a. the practical applications of science.
   b. the aesthetics of science.
   c. literary achievement.

____ 8. Specialty areas in engineering developed as a result of
   a. production demands.
   b. advances in science and technology.
   c. global conflicts.

____ 9. Engineers are likely to be
   a. methodical.
   b. artistic.
   c. disorganized.

____ 10. You can conclude from this article that the field of engineering
   a. is becoming too specialized.
   b. is limited in the number of specialty areas that can be developed.
   c. will probably continue to develop more specialty areas.

SCORE: _____ /10

Name: _____   Date: _____

SWORDFISH

_____ 1. Swordfish are found
    a. in tropical and temperate oceans.
    b. in icy water.
    c. only in the Atlantic Ocean.

_____ 2. Another name for a swordfish is the
    a. herring.
    b. broadbill.
    c. mackerel.

_____ 3. The eyes of a swordfish are
    a. silver.
    b. black.
    c. blue.

_____ 4. Swordfish generally live
    a. close to shore.
    b. offshore.
    c. near islands.

_____ 5. The adult swordfish has
    a. sharp teeth.
    b. no teeth at all.
    c. teeth of different sizes.

_____ 6. Without its sword, the swordfish would find it hard to
    a. swim.
    b. feed.
    c. mate.

_____ 7. It is likely that fishers enjoy catching swordfish because the fish
    a. are easy to catch.
    b. are very colorful.
    c. put up a good fight.

_____ 8. To catch swordfish, a fishing boat should usually stay
    a. close to shore.
    b. offshore.
    c. near islands.

_____ 9. The name _swordfish_ suggests that
    a. swordfish are the only fish with spearlike noses.
    b. all fish have swordlike noses.
    c. the upper jaw of a swordfish is a striking feature.

_____ 10. Swordfish may descend to great depths in search of food, which suggests that
    a. food may be scarce.
    b. swordfish like deep water.
    c. swordfish are solitary hunters.

SCORE: _____ /10

Name: _____   Date: _____

THE BASICS OF BICYCLING

_____ 1. The way a bike is pedaled affects
    a. the height of the seat.
    b. the quality of the ride.
    c. how well it steers.

_____ 2. Pedaling too long in high gears can cause
    a. muscle cramps.
    b. poor traction.
    c. gear stripping.

_____ 3. Peak pedaling efficiency is achieved when a rider pedals
    a. 50 to 60 revolutions per minute.
    b. 70 to 90 revolutions per minute.
    c. 100 to 110 revolutions per minute.

_____ 4. Brakes on multispeed bikes are
    a. hand brakes.
    b. coaster brakes.
    c. foot brakes.

_____ 5. Gears are shifted in order to
    a. maintain pedaling speed.
    b. reduce braking.
    c. keep wheels rolling.

_____ 6. A better-quality ride is achieved by
    a. beginning bike riders.
    b. riders who have practiced biking techniques.
    c. pedaling as fast as possible.

_____ 7. Efficient pedaling is the result of
    a. wearing toe clips.
    b. pushing downward with strain.
    c. a strong downward stroke and upward thrust.

_____ 8. Bikers traveling long distances should use
    a. high gears.
    b. low to moderate gears.
    c. rear wheel locks.

_____ 9. The distance between the seat and the pedal should depend on
    a. how fast a rider pedals.
    b. the style of the bike.
    c. the length of the rider's leg.

_____ 10. You can conclude from the article that compared to one-speed bikes, multispeed bikes are
    a. easier to learn to ride.
    b. harder to pedal.
    c. more efficient.

SCORE: _____ /10

Name: _____ Date: _____

❧ Dragons ❧

_____ 1. Dragon stories have been popular
   a. since prehistoric times.
   b. in the folklore of many countries.
   c. mostly in China and Japan.

_____ 2. Dragon legends may have originated from
   a. prehistoric reptiles.
   b. lizards in the East Indies.
   c. European bats.

_____ 3. The dragon is the emblem of
   a. the former imperial house of China.
   b. current Japanese royalty.
   c. sailors.

_____ 4. Dinosaurs
   a. predate humans on Earth.
   b. appeared after humans.
   c. are mythical creatures.

_____ 5. Certain small lizards in the East Indies are
   a. brightly colored.
   b. able to glide between trees.
   c. known as dinosaurs.

_____ 6. From the article you can conclude that dragons of folklore inspired
   a. worship.
   b. fear.
   c. laughter.

_____ 7. The article wants you to understand that stories about dragons are
   a. factual.
   b. folklore that may have a factual basis.
   c. really stories about dinosaurs.

_____ 8. You can conclude from the article that after Columbus's time, sailors
   a. refused to sail unknown seas.
   b. killed many dragons at sea.
   c. became less fearful of unknown seas.

_____ 9. Today dragons represent
   a. folklore of the past.
   b. creatures to be avoided.
   c. fearful things in life.

_____ 10. Small, harmless lizards in the East Indies are called dragons, which is
   a. practical.
   b. untrue.
   c. ironic.

SCORE: _____ /10

Name: _____   Date: _____

Have a **Prune**

_____ 1. Prunes are
   a. fresh plums.
   b. unripe plums.
   c. dried plums.

_____ 2. The world's best prunes come from
   a. a region in France.
   b. Oregon.
   c. the Middle East.

_____ 3. A prune's powdery coating is called
   a. fur.
   b. bloom.
   c. skin.

_____ 4. Curing prunes results in
   a. hard skins.
   b. uniform moisture content.
   c. dehydration.

_____ 5. Prunes are a good source of
   a. fiber.
   b. protein.
   c. vitamin C.

_____ 6. You can conclude from the article that prunes
   a. have little nutritional value.
   b. are low in sugar.
   c. are considered a healthy food.

_____ 7. It is likely that ancient people dried prunes
   a. in the sun.
   b. using salt water.
   c. in heated dehydrators.

_____ 8. You can conclude that prune packagers are concerned about
   a. how to remove prune pits.
   b. how to package small prunes.
   c. germs on prune skins.

_____ 9. You can conclude that the best prunes are made from plums that are
   a. fully ripe.
   b. green.
   c. not quite ripe.

_____ 10. You can conclude that prunes processed in less than three weeks are
   a. dried in dehydrators.
   b. inferior in quality.
   c. dried in the sun.

SCORE: _____ /10

Name: _____   **Date:** _____

Acid Rain

_____ 1. Acid rain originates from
  a. freezing water.
  b. burning fossil fuels.
  c. the natural environment.

_____ 2. The acidity of liquid solutions is measured by
  a. rainfall amounts.
  b. electrical generators.
  c. the pH factor.

_____ 3. Acid rain is a threat to lakes because
  a. acidity in the water kills virtually all life forms.
  b. it causes water to overflow its banks.
  c. the water becomes too alkaline.

_____ 4. The effects of acid rain are not limited by geographic boundaries because
  a. it rains everywhere.
  b. prevailing winds carry pollutants around the globe.
  c. antipollution equipment is too costly.

_____ 5. It is estimated that by the end of the twentieth century,
  a. up to 100,000 lakes in North America may be destroyed.
  b. up to 300,000 lakes in North America may be destroyed.
  c. up to 500,000 lakes in North America may be destroyed.

_____ 6. You can conclude from the article that acid rain
  a. is a problem that cannot be solved by one country alone.
  b. can never be eliminated.
  c. is the most important problem facing the world.

_____ 7. You can conclude that the destruction of lakes by acid rain has been the most severe where
  a. there is the most industry.
  b. the level of acidity in rainfall is the highest.
  c. wind is the strongest.

_____ 8. You can conclude that lakes are destroyed by acid rain because
  a. plants and animals that live in the water die.
  b. acidity kills the water.
  c. surrounding vegetation is killed.

_____ 9. You can conclude that the only way to reverse the effects of acid rain is
  a. through education.
  b. with antipollution equipment.
  c. by measuring water acidity.

_____ 10. The most devastating effects of acid rain may eventually be
  a. loss of all rivers, lakes, and streams.
  b. destruction of great monuments.
  c. loss of human life.

SCORE: _____ /10